ONCE UPON A MATTRESS
LIFE IN BED

Written and Illustrated By:
Martin Riskin

30 29 28 27 26 25 24 23 22 21 20 19 18 17 16 15 14 13 12 11 10 9 8 7 6 5 4 3 2 1

Ivory Tower Publishing Co., Inc.
125 Walnut St., P.O. Box 9132, Watertown, MA 02272-9132
Telephone #: (617) 923-1111   Fax #: (617) 923-8839

Bed [bed] n. A soft place with floral sheets where you lie down and someone puts their cold feet on your back.

Aside from the sexual issues which have been thoroughly covered in libraries of other books, what's the big secret about what people really do in bed? That's what this book is all about. People don't leave their baggage at the bedroom door, they drag it to bed with them. Bed is simply life with pillows and blankets.

Most of us start out in one of those little baskets in the maternity ward, the ones you see from behind the big glass window when you're visiting someone who has just had a baby. Your identity is determined by a pink or blue blanket, and a piece of masking tape has your name scrawled on it. You do a lot of spasmodic kicking which can be loosely translated as "Get me the hell out of here," and "Where's my damn nipple?"

Once they get you home, they put you in a <u>Crib</u>. There's a little more room here, but right away you notice the bars and the distinct crinkle of the rubber sheet under you. This means they don't trust you or your bladder. They try to distract you by filling your crib with soft, stuffed animals and a jiggling mobile toy that's just out of your reach. A couple of years pass and you graduate into a contraption called a <u>Training Bed</u>. It looks like a bed, but the bars are still there, and since your crib smelled like a bus station restroom, the rubber sheets made the move with you.

...They don't trust you or your bladder.

WEINSWIG'S COMPLAINT

...You turn the corner into childhood. Now, your bed becomes a place where fantasies rule; a place where pillows become wild horses or villains to punch, and mattresses make quite adequate trampolines. Bed manufacturers know this and make beds that look like racing cars or gingerbread cottages.

Every night Irwin would put on his black snow shoes and his father's belt.

On his 7th birthday, my friend Irwin Weinswig got a fire engine bed. It had a bright red headboard with gold letters and numbers on it, spelling out "Playville Fire Department 17". A steering wheel was attached to the footboard and a real rubber wheel adorned each leg.

Every night, Irwin would put on his black snow shoes and his father's belt. With black, electrical tape, he attached the various tools of the fireman's trade: a ladle, a pencil and a beach pail. This is how Irwin slept for years. I thought he was the luckiest kid on the planet. Irwin is now in the wholesale fruit business.

From here on, as your life turns each corner, the personality of your bed changes right with you. The Adolescent Bed is complete with stuffed animals, posters, dirty books stuffed under the mattress and basketball-sized dust clumps underneath. Then comes the Mating Bed when your bed becomes a pawn in the elaborate rituals to attract a member of the opposite sex into it. Here, a well-placed mirror, satin sheets and a decent dab of perfume here and there will serve you well. Onto the Marriage Bed, with its paisley pillows and down comforter. Next comes the Parental Bed, complete with cookie crumbs and a forgotten plastic robot. Then the Geriatric Bed, that folds up like a sandwich at the push of a control button. And finally, the Death Bed, where you whisper your last "Screw Them All" into your clergyman's ear. I wouldn't worry too much about the afterlife either, because if nothing else, there'll probably be a damn good bed there. What else could you hope for?

"HIS LAST WORD'S WERE... 'TELL THE INSURANCE COMPANY TO TAKE A LONG LEAP OFF A SHORT PIER.'"

A TALE OF TWO PILLOWS

I have a confession to make... It's probably a remnant from my childhood days when I was in love with a scruffy, old security blanket. The truth is, I have my own pillow. I mean, I have a serious relationship with this pillow. It squishes down in just the right way and it fits my head perfectly. I have to admit that I really love this pillow.

**The truth is...
I love my pillow.**

A TALE OF TWO PILLOWS

When I travel, I try like hell to take the pillow with me, telling myself that it will help me sleep better in strange surroundings.

It's not an easy thing to pack a pillow in a suitcase, especially if you're trying to hide it from your wife. My wife hates my pillow, by the way. She feels that I am more affectionate to it than I am to her. This is unfortunately true. She fails to realize that my pillow a) never puts cold feet at the base of my back, b) does not fart in bed and c) rarely stabs me with a toenail.

When I travel, I try like hell to take my pillow with me.

A TALE OF TWO PILLOWS

I was forced to carry my pillow fully exposed on the elevator.

A pillow will take up most of a suitcase, so I usually stuff mine into a smaller travel bag or carry it separately in a plastic store bag so it looks like I just bought it. On one occasion, just after checking into a hotel, I was forced to carry my pillow, fully exposed, under my arm for a reason I fail to recall right now. But I was on an elevator on the way up to my room. I noticed there was another guy on the elevator and he also had a pillow.

A TALE OF TWO PILLOWS

But his pillow had its own zippered plastic bag. This guy stared at me and my pillow with a wry, inquisitive smile. Trying to dilute some of my embarrassment, I blurted out "Allergy." The guy smiled and looked down at his pillow and said "Dwinky." I wanted to sink through the floor. The elevator door mercifully opened and I made a rapid, red-faced exit, even though I was three floors below my room. My pillow and I ascended the rest of the way in the privacy of the cinder block lined stairway.

I made a rapid, red-faced exit into the privacy of the cinder block stairwell.

BIG PHILOSOPHICAL THOUGHTS TO HELP YOU FALL ASLEEP AT NIGHT

PHILOSOPHICAL QUESTION #1

You know those little bottles of typing correction fluid you can buy in a stationery store? If each bottle contains approximately 1 oz. of fluid and costs, let's say, 69¢, how many bottles would it take to paint the outside of an average suburban eight room house? And what would it cost?

PILLOWSPEAK

SHE: What are you doing?

HE: Looking for something in the bottom bureau drawer.

SHE: What's so funny?

HE: I just found a picture of you in a bathing suit with a bunch of droolers.

SHE: I was popular then.

HE: What ever happened to those geeks you hung around with?

SHE: ...I married the third one in from the left.

"I'M TOILET TRAINED, TRUE... BUT NOT HIGHLY TOILET TRAINED."

PILLOWSPEAK

SHE: Oh look,... a bird's nest outside under the sill.

HE: Get me a broom.

SHE: No. Wait... there are baby birds in the nest.

HE: So now we're gonna have a kindergarten under our window until December.

SHE: They're so cute and helpless.

HE: ...Too bad they're not constipated.

"I LIKED YOU BETTER AS A FROG."

PILLOWSPEAK

SHE: I am mortified.

HE: What now?

SHE: Your 8-year-old son found my sanitary napkins in the back of the closet. He took them to school in his knapsack and distributed them to his friends.

HE: Maybe he's just curious.

SHE: How can I ever face those children again?

HE: ...Tell them they're your shoulderpads.

"THIS IS YOUR 'ON THE SPOT' REPORTER, CYNTHIA TURKELSTEIN..
COMING TO YOU FROM BED."

PILLOWSPEAK

HE: What was that?

SHE: Nothing.

HE: You farted didn't you?

SHE: I most certainly did not!

HE: I thought ladies never cut wind in public.

SHE: This is not in public, and you are an insensitive animal.

HE: Another feminist myth blown to smithereens.

BABY SLEEP

Whoever invented cribs knew what they were doing, and it's a lucky thing babies sleep in them because babies really travel when they sleep. (See illustration on the opposite page.) I think if you put a sleeping baby down in the middle of New York City, by morning, the baby would be in New Jersey.

By morning, the baby would be in New Jersey.

THE NIGHT OF THE BABY

PILLOWSPEAK

SHE: When was the last time you took a shower?

HE: This morning, why?

SHE: Did you use an antiperspirant?

HE: Yeah.

SHE: I mean did you use an anti-perspirant, not a deodorant?

HE: I used the stuff in the medicine cabinet. What's the difference?

SHE: An antiperspirant stops the odor and a deodorant just covers it up, that's the difference.

HE: So report me to the underarm police.

"FOR PETE'S SAKE... CAN'T A MAN HIBERNATE IN PEACE THESE DAYS?"

PILLOWSPEAK

SHE: There's a mosquito buzzing around in here.

HE: Tell him to buzz quieter.

SHE: It's not funny,... mosquitoes carry sleeping sickness and malaria.

HE: If he bites us and we get sleeping sickness, at least we'd get some sleep.

"CAN SOMEBODY PRESS THREE?"

PILLOWSPEAK

SHE: There's a spider on the ceiling.

HE: So?

SHE: Would you please get up and get rid of him?

HE: Why, the spider is just sitting there quietly?

SHE: After we fall asleep, he'll drop down on the bed.

HE: We've got a king-sized bed, there's room for all of us.

PILLOWSPEAK

SHE: Today, I cleaned out your closet.

HE: There was nothing wrong with my closet.

SHE: I took all your old ties and I'm recycling them.

HE: Recycling them?

SHE: I'm going to use them to hang my flower pots.

HE: This weekend, I'm going to use a couple of your old panty girdles to wash my truck.

"IT'S NOT A NAP... IT'S EXTREMELY LOW IMPACT AEROBICS."

LIFE UNDER THE BED

Shmutz [shm-ootz] n. An assorted collection of dusty debris from under your bed.

MOST COMMON SHMUTZ FOUND UNDER TYPICAL BED

 KEY TO WHO KNOWS WHAT

 PETRIFIED CAT BOWEL MOVEMENT

 CRUMPLED UP TISSUE FROM 1991 FLU SEASON

 COMMON DUST SHLOGS

 COINS (NOTHING OVER A DIME)

 ASSORTED PUBIC HAIR

 CAT'S WHISKER

 HAIRPIN FROM THE STONE AGE

 BELLY BUTTON LINT

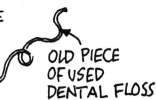 OLD PIECE OF USED DENTAL FLOSS

 OLD PIECE OF FAMOUS AMOS COOKIE

 TOENAIL CLIPPINGS

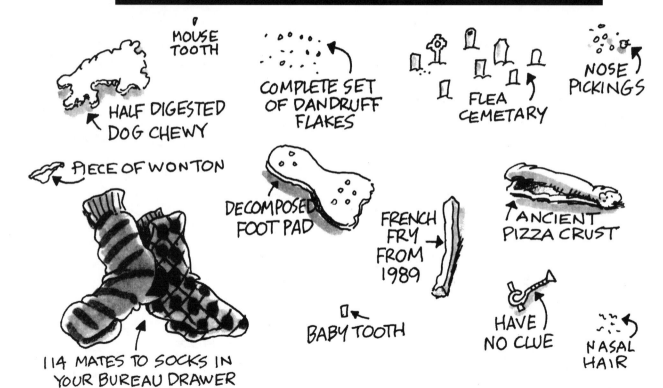

...AND EVEN MORE SHMUTZ

OLD UNDERWEAR

EYELASH

DRIED ZIT

TV GUIDE FROM THE 70'S

CONFUSED SPIDER

CRUSTED OVER SPIT-UP

CHICKEN FEATHER

BABY SNEAKER (Baby just entered college)

SPLINTER FROM THE TIME YOU STRAIGHTENED THE BEDBOARDS

CHOOSING UP SIDES

It must be scrawled deeply within some obscure paragraph of the Dead Sea Scrolls. It's the law that determines who gets the side of the bed next to the window, the television set and the thermostat controls, and who gets the side with the mattress lump and the alarm clock.

Who decides who gets the side next to the window?

CHOOSING UP SIDES

**I have an unobstructed
view of the hamper.**

I don't remember exactly how it came to be, but all I know is that I'm in charge of the alarm clock. My wife, on the other hand, has a delightful, eastern-exposure, window-side position. The sun rises on her side and sets on my side. She has domain over the TV remote, the electric blanket and the thermostat temperature controls, with direct access to the tissue box. I have an unobstructed view of the hamper.

CHOOSING UP SIDES

Within easy arms reach on her side is her night table. She calls it a night table, but, to me, it's really a "toolbox". In the top drawer, there are at least a dozen different kinds of tweezer things, ominous little contraptions that squeeze, pluck, crimp and twist zits. Then there are the hair rollers, whole communities of them, pink ones with spines on them, white ones with holes and blue ones with teeth. And the library of old <u>Woman's Day</u> magazines she's saving. Remember the issue that showed us how to make jewelry out of turkey bones leftover from Thanksgiving 1972? It's there.

**She calls it a night table.
I call it a toolbox.**

CHOOSING UP SIDES

The spaghetti tangle of old TV earplug wires.

And who can forget the nail clippers, nail files, emery boards and dental floss nestled among the old bra clip graveyard? Not to mention the vast spaghetti tangle of portable radio and TV earplug wires from the days when couples actually felt bad about disturbing each other.

PILLOWSPEAK

HE: Why do you have to pluck your facial hair in bed every night?

SHE: For the same reason you have to pick your toes.

HE: Point.

"WE INTERRUPT THIS PROGRAM TO BRING YOU THIS NEWS BULLETIN... YOUR HUSBAND HAS STASHED A PENTHOUSE MAGAZINE IN THE BOTTOM BUREAU DRAWER."

PILLOWSPEAK

HE: Your feet are freezing!

SHE: ...And the base of your back is nice and toasty.

HE: We do make sort of a good team, don't we?

SHE: My feet and your spine... a marriage made in heaven.

PILLOWSPEAK

SHE: Why are you wearing your slippers in bed?

HE: Because I heard the cat garp up a hair ball on the floor before, and I don't feel like stepping on it if I have to get up in the night.

SHE: So you left it for me to clean up?

HE: Don't worry about it.

SHE: I worry about your inconsideration.

HE: I just rolled over on top of it.

"YOU CAN REBUILD YOUR FORT LATER, ARTHUR...
RIGHT NOW I NEED TO MAKE THE BED."

PILLOWSPEAK

SHE: Let's discuss.

HE: I was just about to drop off.

SHE: We never talk to each other .
Other couples talk in bed.

HE: So talk.

SHE: What shall we talk about?

HE: Let's talk about ways for me to
get an uninterrupted night's
sleep.

"THE PILKERSON'S ARE AT IT AGAIN...!"

PHILOSOPHICAL QUESTION #2

What if you never had to sleep? Over the span of a 75 years average lifetime, if you slept an average of 8 hours a day, how much time could you save? Now, if you got a job that paid $7.65/hour, how much money could you earn over that period?

BIG PHILOSOPHICAL THOUGHTS TO HELP YOU FALL ASLEEP AT NIGHT

PHILOSOPHICAL QUESTION #3

Take your average stewardess. If she worked two flights a day and each flight carried 137 passengers, how many times would she have to say... "Bye, now," in one month, before she went insane?

YOU AND YOUR BLANKET

The time has come to talk about blankets. Blankets are for covering yourself during sleep periods. When used in this way, blankets are usually a good thing.

If you're sleeping alone, you can have your own way with a blanket. Besides covering yourself with it, you can squinch it between your legs, wrap it around your head or kick it onto the floor, and no one will say a word. If you're not sleeping alone, possession becomes 9/10 of the law regarding blankets.

HOW TO GAIN POSSESSION OF A BLANKET DURING THE NIGHT WITHOUT THEM EVER CATCHING ON.

Wait until the other person falls asleep. Then, in one swift, strong motion, yank the blanket out from under the sleeping person like a lounge magician yanking a tablecloth out from under a fully set table. The second way is to slowly acquire the blanket, square foot by square foot, over a period of time. Either way, they'll never catch on.

THE NIGHT OF THE BLANKETS

PILLOWSPEAK

SHE: ...Ow!

HE: What?

SHE: You stabbed me with your toenails.

HE: Sorry.

SHE: ...So cut them.

HE: Now?

SHE: Yes, right now... I won't stay in the same bed with a man who has disgusting toenails!

HE: Let me get this right... You'll stay in bed with a dog who licks his testicles and a hair-puking cat, but my toenails are too tough to deal with?

SHE: I always thought you were a couple rungs higher up the evolutionary ladder, but I was wrong.

PILLOWSPEAK

SHE: Where's the cat?

HE: Don't know.

SHE: Is the cat in or out?

HE: Out I think.

SHE: I can't sleep if the cat is out.

HE: Why?

SHE: Rabid raccoons.

HE: When was the last time you saw any rabid raccoons?

SHE: It was in the paper.

HE: A husband who murdered his wife for annoying him was also in the paper.

SHE: It's not funny.

HE: Who's laughing?

SHE: Find the cat and get her in so I can sleep.

HE: Cats are nocturnal creatures. They hunt mice at night.

SHE: I think I heard a mouse screaming.

PILLOWSPEAK

SHE: I have an itch.

HE: Where?

SHE: Under my shoulder blade.

HE: Here?

SHE: Up a little.

HE: There?

SHE: To the right, and down a teensy bit.

HE: Your right or my right?

SHE: I don't know, I can't think in reverse.

HE: Why don't I scratch your whole damn back and hopefully I'll hit the spot sooner or later.

SHE: Go.

"WE'RE THE MILNERS, FROM NEXT DOOR... AND WE WERE WONDERING WHEN YOU WERE GOING TO PULL DOWN YOUR BEDROOM SHADES?"

PILLOWSPEAK

SHE: I'm cold.

HE: It's not cold in here.

SHE: I don't care, I'm cold.

HE: Do you want me to build a fire under the bed?

SHE: No, Mr. Sensitive. I just need to be held.

HE: Why didn't you just say that in the first place?

SHE: You'll never get it, will you?

HE: Get what?

"I'M IN HERE, ...SOMEWHERE."

SLEEP POSITIONS

What can you assume about people who never move when they sleep? You can assume they are dead. And what can you tell about folks who sleep sprawled across a bed like a road-kill carcass? Well, you can probably tell that as soon as those people fall asleep, they're on the move. And move they do, all night, all around, until you hit them with the clock radio. Then they stop. Then they wake up and say, "What?" You tell them they were moving, so you hit them. Before you finish saying it, they're asleep and moving again.

Scientists have high-minded theories about Alpha Sleep, Rem Sleep and different levels of consciousness, but simply, people look silly when they sleep. The illustrations on the next few pages depict some of the more common sleep positions. See if you can find yourself.

SLEEP POSITIONS

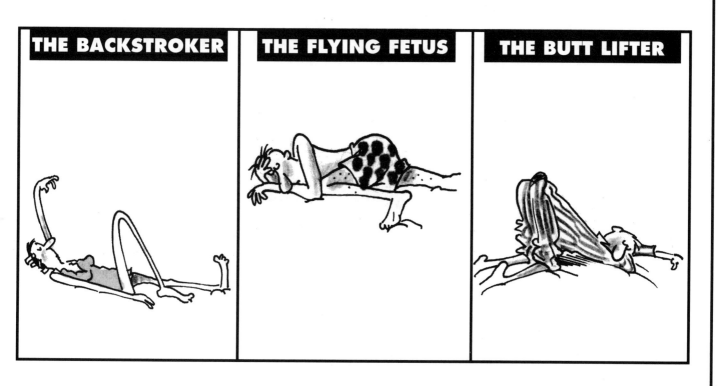

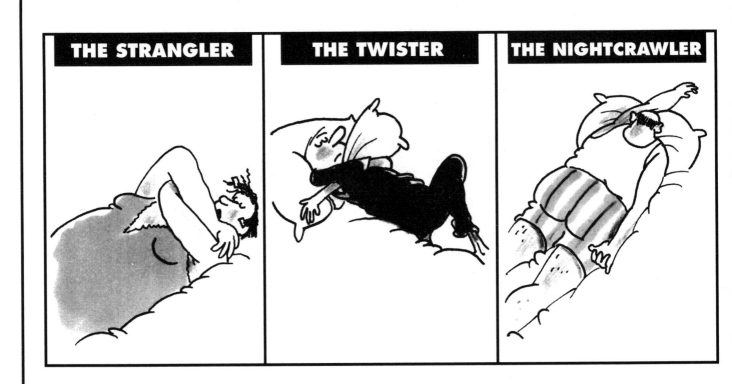

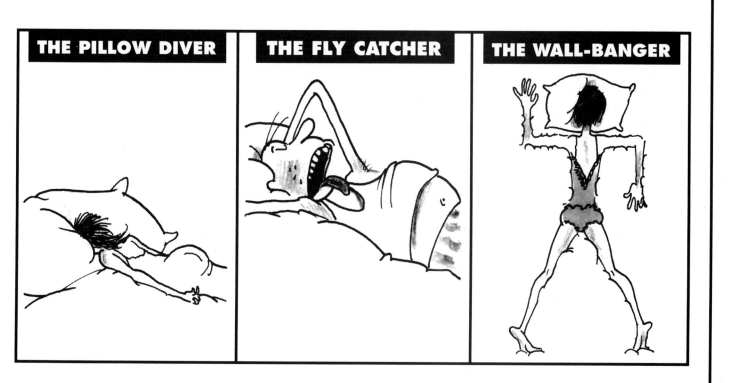

PILLOWSPEAK

SHE: What are you doing?

HE: Coming to bed.

SHE: What time is it?

HE: 1 o'clock.

SHE: I can't sleep.

HE: Why?

SHE: You woke me up.

HE: How come you can sleep with the TV blaring in your face like a fog horn, but me unbuttoning my shirt wakes you up?

SHE: The TV is entertaining, you're not.

"THE BURGLAR I MET IN THE KITCHEN, WANTS TO KNOW
IF WE HAVE ANY TARTAR SAUCE...?"

PILLOWSPEAK

SHE: Is it hot in here or is it just me?

HE: It's just you.

"MS. FELZNER, SEND IN MY BLANKIE."

PILLOWSPEAK

SHE: Are you awake?

HE: No.

SHE: I'm wide awake.

HE: Why?

SHE: I had a dream.

HE: What dream?

SHE: A serial killer came in through the cellar window and cut up the cat with a scissors.

HE: Think about what we'll save on cat food alone.

SHE: Go down and check the cellar windows.

"I THINK HE LIKES IT...!"

PILLOWSPEAK

SHE: Is it possible for you to stop?

HE: Stop what?

SHE: Your incessant channel surfing.

HE: I can't stop.

SHE: Why do you do it?

HE: Because I might miss something good.

SHE: Give me the remote.

HE: You shut it off!

SHE: What are you doing now?

HE: Channel surfing your tush.

SHE: Here's the remote back.

HE: Where's the remote?

SHE: I don't know.

HE: You were using it 5 minutes ago.

SHE: Can't you just enjoy television without surfing up and down the channels?

HE: No.

SHE: You have a sickness, do you know that?

HE: I'm sick of the Home Shopping Network. That's for sure.

"WE DON'T CUDDLE ANYMORE."

THE WELL-DRESSED BED

Everyone out there who thinks that buying a house is the most complicated and the most important purchase one makes in a lifetime, ...raise your hands.

Think again, mortgage breath.

Beds probably started out on some ancient plain, as just a pile of well-placed grass to keep the rocks out of an enterprising Neanderthal's back. Since then, things have gotten progressively worse. A fully equipped bed in the 90's can cost from $2,500 to $3,500. That's a lot of grass.

Beds probably started out as a pile of grass on some ancient plain.

THE WELL-DRESSED BED

LET'S GO TO THE BED STORE...

YOU: I need a bed.

THEM: Bunk, water, single, twin, double, queen, king or football field?

YOU: I just need a bed, not a plot plan.

THEM: Let's start with the frame, headboard, footboard, box spring, conventional or Hollywood, colonial, traditional or campaign, wood, wood veneer, cherry, oak or maple?

YOU: Don't know, don't know... don't know.

THEM: Next is the box spring—wood frame, steel, steel reinforced, corner joisted or cross braced?... Covered with cotton twill, padded or canvas faced?

YOU: I feel dizzy.

THEM: Now the mattress... posture-perfect, coiled wire or... (Salesman takes out a laundry list of mattress names, all beginning with Ortho, Sacro or Chiro.)

YOU: I need some fresh air. (You make a break for the front door and the mall, but you're intercepted by a large bottomed lady with glasses on a chain and a pencil stuck in her wig.)

...CORNER JOISTED OR CROSS BRACED?... COTTON TWILL PADDED OR CANVAS FACED?

I'M GETTING NAUSEOUS.

THE WELL-DRESSED BED

LET'S GO TO THE BED STORE CONTINUED...

THEM: I'm Charlotte, your bedding counselor.

YOU: I need help, Charlotte.

THEM: That's why I'm here.

YOU: Help me, Charlotte.

THEM: Let's start with the box spring cover, sham and dust ruffle...

YOU: (After a horrible hour and a half of Charlotte badgering you about bottom covers, top sheets, pads, cases, blankets, puffs, mattress pads, pillow covers, comforters, bed spreads and decorative pillows for when the real pillows are not being used... You surrender $3,000 and crawl like a beaten dog out onto the cool, waxed tiles of the mall.)

We should've used Charlotte during Desert Storm.

I crawled like a beaten dog onto the cool, waxed tiles of the mall.

SHEETS & PILLOWCASE COLORS MEN HAVE NEVER HEARD OF

Mauve	Peacock	Nutmeg
Puce	Colonial Ivory	Mint
Magenta	Smoked Rose	Lemon Chiffon
Ecru	Melon	Periwinkle
Lavender	Champagne	Sonata Pink
Daffodil	Coriander	Prairie Gold

PILLOWSPEAK

HE: The baby is crying.

SHE: The baby needs to be changed.

HE: So change her.

SHE: I changed her last night.

HE: But I changed her four hours ago.

SHE: I'm very comfortable... If I get up now, I'll never find this position again.

HE: I've been finessed.

PILLOWSPEAK

SHE: I can't sleep with the air conditioner on.

HE: But it's muggy as hell in here.

SHE: I don't care. When the air conditioner is on, you can't hear anything.

HE: What do you want to hear?

SHE: Burglars.

HE: Why didn't you say so. I'd much rather be sweaty and listen for burglars anytime than be cool and comfortable.

"IS THAT SUPPOSED TO MEAN YOU WANT ME TO TURN UP THE ELECTRIC BLANKET A NOTCH?"

PILLOWSPEAK

SHE: Someone is licking my toes.

HE: It's the dog.

SHE: You used to do romantic things, remember?

HE: Yeah... But I bought a dog to do the tougher jobs. Remember?

SHE: How can I forget?

"MY HUSBAND THINKS THESE SHEETS ARE LOVELY... BUT HE WANTS TO KNOW IF YOU HAVE ANY WITH TOOLS ON THEM?"

PILLOWSPEAK

SHE: The alarm... Get the alarm!

HE: Which button shuts it off?

SHE: The middle one.

HE: That's the radio.

SHE: I said the middle one!

HE: That's the snooze bar.

SHE: SHUT IT OFF!... For Pete's sake.

CRASH, CRUNCH.

SHE: Why did you do that?

HE: It's off isn't it?

"YOU DON'T SEE THE LITTLE FISHIES BOTHERING THEIR DADDY EVERY FIVE MINUTES FOR WATER, DO YOU, KEVIN?"

BIG THOUGHTS ABOUT SLEEP

A big thought occurred to me while I was writing this book. Excluding bedtime, I almost never can sleep when and where I want to. For example, I would love to be able to sleep on a plane, but, to this day, I have never fallen asleep on a plane. My theory is that people would like to sleep on planes, but can't. So, what do the marketing geniuses who work for the airlines do? They give us peanuts. Give us beds, you idiots!

I'm drifting too far from my original point which was not being able to sleep when you'd like to, and visa-versa. These two lists should clear things up, or confuse you some more.

"I almost never can sleep when and where I want to."

PLACES YOU'D LIKE TO SLEEP BUT NEVER CAN

1. 30 Hour Trans-Pacific flight.
2. During a root canal.
3. In the woods, in a pup tent, on an air mattress.
4. Overnight on Aunt Sophie's couch.
5. On a waterbed.

ACME WATERBED

PLACES YOU SHOULDN'T SLEEP BUT ALWAYS DO

1. On the beach just before you put on the sunscreen.
2. One quarter of the way into that good movie you forgot to videotape.
3. In the middle of "The Little Engine That Could," you were reading for the eighth time to your wide-awake kid.
4. 11 a.m. on the New Jersey Turnpike.
5. The beginning of the sermon.

THOSE WHO WAKE UP AND THOSE WHO DON'T

Let's put all the blame on metabolism, because when it comes to waking up, there are two kinds of people: those who wake up and those who don't.

First, there are the UP AND AT 'EM types. You know them, they're the people who jump up at the first buzz of the alarm, filled with Joie de Vie. They're out of the bed and into their stretching exercises instantly. Then it's a bound and a leap into the shower, followed by some very bad singing. After brushing and flossing and all polished up and cologned, it's into the kitchen for juice, decaffeinated coffee, oatmeal and vitamins. Then it's sunrise seminar, some news and out the front door to form those miserable traffic snarls on the way to work.

The second group of people, The PILLOW CLUTCHERS, don't really wake up at all. After copious pleading, prodding and yelling, they very reluctantly crawl, limply and reluctantly, from the warm womb of the quilt to the cold bedroom floor.
The UP AND AT 'EM's are good until about 3 p.m., then things begin to unravel for them. By 7 p.m., they're ironing handkerchiefs for the next day and by 9 p.m., you could cover their eyes with pennies because they're corpses.

By 4 p.m., the PILLOW CLUTCHERS are just waking up and are ready to rule the night. They're the people who populate the lounges, watch all the late night movies and call all those 900 numbers.

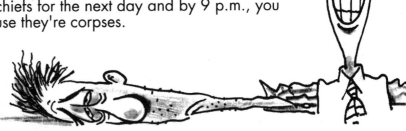

TOP 10 THINGS MEN WOULD LIKE TO SEE ON THEIR SHEETS AND PILLOWCASES

10. Rosin Bags

9. Diner Food

8. Stock Quotations

7. Spare Ribs

6. Truck Logos

5. Tattoos

4. Motorcycles

3. Babes

2. Pit Bulls

...And the most popular thing men want to see on their bed linens is...

1. Tools

PILLOWSPEAK

HE: What's the matter?

SHE: I can't get comfortable.

HE: Why can't you?

SHE: I keep thinking about cocoa and a buttered muffin.

HE: We don't have any cocoa or muffins in the house.

SHE: I know...

HE: You're not suggesting that I get up, get dressed, and go out into the freezing rain to some God-forsaken 24-hour convenience store populated with child molesters and gunmen, are you?

SHE: Of course not... How selfish of me.

HE: What kind of muffin do you want?

"TONIGHT... YOU COME TO MY SIDE."

PILLOWSPEAK

SHE: How many pillows do you have?

HE: Three.

SHE: Why would a grown man need three pillows?

HE: One is for my head.

SHE: OK, I'll give you that one.

HE: The other pillow is for my leg.

SHE: What's wrong with your leg?

HE: Nothing. It just feels comfortable to put my leg up on it.

SHE: What about the third pillow?

HE: It's for my arm.

SHE: What's wrong with your arm?

HE: It just feels good.

SHE: So why don't you adopt the three pillows, then you'd have the best of both worlds; me to cook and clean for you all day, and you could sleep with the pillows at night!

"FOR HEAVEN'S SAKE, MIRIAM... WILL YOU STOP COMPLAINING AND JUST HOLD STILL."

SECRET OBNOXIOUSLY-CUTE NAMES FOR YOUR PILLOW

Snugger	Gypper	Boinger	Numby
Boofy	Dumby	Floppy	Hugs
Bunky	Tweaky	Squeaks	Mugs
Snorfy	Winky	Pussums	Mumbly
Puffer	Cuddlebug	Waffles	Snubbins
Fluffer	Huggle	Snowflake	Marshmallow
Squishy	Snoozy	Larry	Madonna

Other books we publish are available at many fine stores. If you can't find them, send directly to us. $7.00 postpaid

2400-How To Have Sex On Your Birthday. Finding a partner, special birthday sex positions and much more.

2402-Confessions From The Bathroom. There are things in this book that happen to all of us that none of us ever talk about, like the Gas Station Dump, the Corn Niblet Dump and more.

2403-The Good Bonking Guide. Great new term for doing "you know what". Bonking in the dark, bonking all night long, improving your bonking, and everything else you ever wanted to know.

2407-40 Happens. When being out of prune juice ruins your whole day and you realize anyone with the energy to do it on a weeknight must be a sex maniac.

2408-30 Happens. When you take out a lifetime membership at your health club, and you still wonder when the baby fat will finally disappear.

2409-50 Happens. When you remember when "made in Japan" meant something that didn't work, and you can't remember what you went to the top of the stairs for.

2411-The Geriatric Sex Guide. It's not his mind that needs expanding; and you're in the mood now, but by the time you're naked, you won't be!

2412-Golf Shots. What excuses to use to play through first, ways to distract your opponent, and when and where a true golfer is willing to play.

2416-The Absolutely Worst Fart Book. The First Date Fart, The Lovers' Fart, The Doctor's Exam Room Fart and more.

2417-Women Over 30 Are Better Because... Their nightmares about exams are starting to fade and their handbags can sustain life for about a week with no outside support whatsoever.

2418-9 Months In The Sac. Pregnancy through the eyes of the baby, such as: why do pregnant women have to go to the bathroom as soon as they get to the store, and why does baby start doing aerobics when it's time to sleep?

2419-Cucumbers Are Better Than Men Because... Cucumbers are always ready when you are and cucumbers will never hear "yes, yes" when you're saying "NO, NO."

2421-Honeymoon Guide. The Advantages Of Undressing With The Light On (it's easier to undo a bra) to What Men Want Most (being able to sleep right afterwards and not talk about love).

2422-Eat Yourself Healthy. Calories only add up if the food is consumed at a table and green M&M's are full of the same vitamins found in broccoli.

2423-Is There Sex After 40? She liked you better when the bulge above your waist was in your trousers. He thinks wife-swapping means getting someone else to cook for you.

2424-Is There Sex After 50? Going to bed early means a chance to catch up on your reading and you miss making love quietly so as not to wake the kids.

2425-Women Over 40 Are Better Because... No matter how many sit-ups they do, they can't recapture their 17-year-old body—but they can find something attractive in any 21-year-old guy.

2426-Women Over 50 Are Better Because... They will be amused if you take them parking, and they know that being alone is better than being with someone they don't like.

2427-You Know You're Over The Hill When... All your stories have bored most acquaintances several times over. You're resigned to being overweight after trying every diet that has come along in the last 15 years.

2428-Beer Is Better Than Women Because (Part II)... A beer doesn't get upset if you call it by the wrong name; and after several beers, you can go to sleep without having to talk about love.

2429-Married To A Computer. You fondle it daily, you keep in touch when you're travelling and you stare at it a lot without understanding it.

2430-Is There Sex After 30? He thinks foreplay means parading around nude in front of the mirror, holding his stomach in; and she found that the quickest way to get rid of a date is to start talking about commitment.

2431-Happy Birthday You Old Fart! You spend less and less time between visits to a toilet, your back goes out more than you do and you leave programming the VCR to people under 25.

2432-Big Weenies. Why some people have big weenies while other people have teenie weenies; as well as the kinds of men who possess a member, a rod and a wang—and more!

2433-Games You Can Play With Your Pussy. Why everyone should have a pussy; how to give a pussy a bath (grease the sides of the tub so it can't claw its way out); and more!

2434-Sex And Marriage. What wives want out of marriage—romance, respect and a Bloomingdale's chargecard; what husbands want out of marriage—to be allowed to sleep after sex.

2435-Baby's First Year. How much will it cost, secrets of midnight feedings, do diapers really cause leprosy and other vital info for parents.

2436-How To Love A New Yorker. You love a New Yorker by pretending to understand their accent, sharing a parking space and realizing they look at "Out of Towners" as new income.

2437-The Retirement Book. Updates the retiree on Early Bird Specials, finding their bifocals and remembering things like paying for the book.

2438-Dog Farts. They do it under the table, in front of the TV, and after devouring some animal they caught in the yard. This book describes them all.

2439-Handling His Midlife Crisis. By treating him like a child when he wants to feel young again and consoling him when he goes from bikinis to boxer shorts.

2440-How To Love A Texan. You love a Texan by agreeing that their chili is just a mite hot, humoring them when they refer to their half acre as a ranch and rushing to help when their belt buckle sets off a security alarm.

2441-Bedtime Stories for your Kitty. Kitties love a story before bedtime and this book guarantees to keep their attention; Goldisocks and the 3 Teddy Bears, The 3 Little Kittens, and more.

2442-Bedtime Stories for your Doggie. This book of tales will keep big doggies as well as puppies entranced every night with stories like The 3 Billy Dogs Gruff, The Little Doggie That Could and many more.

2443-60 With Sizzle! When your kids start to look middle-aged and when your hearing is perfect if everyone would just stop mumbling.

Ivory Tower Publishing Co., Inc., 125 Walnut St., P.O. Box 9132, Watertown, MA 02272-9132   Tel: (617) 923-1111